Landmark
Events in
American
History

Building the
Panama Canal

Dale Anderson

WORLD ALMANAC® LIBRARY

Please visit our web site at: www.worldalmanaclibrary.com
For a free color catalog describing World Almanac® Library's list of high-quality
books and multimedia programs, call 1-800-848-2928 (USA) or 1-800-387-3178
(Canada). World Almanac® Library's fax: (414) 332-3567.

Library of Congress Cataloging-in-Publication Data

Anderson, Dale, 1953-
    Building the Panama Canal / by Dale Anderson.
       p. cm. — (Landmark events in American history)
    Includes bibliographical references and index.
    ISBN 0-8368-5394-6 (lib. bdg.)
    ISBN 0-8368-5422-5 (softcover)
    1. Panama Canal (Panama)—History—Juvenile literature. 2. Canals—Panama—
Design and construction—History—Juvenile literature. 3. Canal Zone—History—
Juvenile literature. I. Title. II. Series.
    F1569.C2A57   2004
    972.87'5—dc22
                                                   2004042020

First published in 2005 by
World Almanac® Library
330 West Olive Street, Suite 100
Milwaukee, WI 53212 USA

Copyright © 2005 by World Almanac® Library.

Produced by Discovery Books
Editor: Sabrina Crewe
Designer and page production: Sabine Beaupré
Photo researcher: Sabrina Crewe
Maps and diagrams: Stefan Chabluk
World Almanac® Library editorial direction: Mark J. Sachner
World Almanac® Library editor: Jenette Donovan Guntly
World Almanac® Library art direction: Tammy West
World Almanac® Library production: Jessica Morris

Photo credits: Corbis: cover, pp. 5, 10, 12, 14, 15, 16, 21, 24, 28, 29, 30, 33, 34, 36,
39, 40, 42, 43; Library of Congress: pp. 4, 20, 23, 25, 26, 27, 31 (both), 35, 37, 38, 41;
North Wind Picture Archives: pp. 6, 7, 8, 9, 11, 17, 18, 19, 22.

Printed in Canada

1 2 3 4 5 6 7 8 9 08 07 06 05 04

Contents

Introduction

A Marvel of Engineering

The Panama **Canal** is one of the engineering marvels of the world. It took tens of thousands of workers to build the canal, which stretches about 50 miles (80 kilometers) to connect the Atlantic and Pacific Oceans.

Work began on the canal in 1905 and was completed in 1914. The Panama Canal was a project of the U.S. government, but there had been earlier plans by other nations and various groups. From 1880 to 1889, a French company worked on a canal in Panama, but the project failed.

The Lock System

The canal has six pairs of **locks**, or passages in which the water level changes so that ships can be moved between waterways at different heights. Three pairs of locks on the Atlantic side of the canal raise or lower ships 85 feet (26 meters). Three pairs on the Pacific side do the same work. The locks are in pairs so that ships traveling in opposite directions can be raised or lowered at the same time.

The locks on the Panama Canal are like giant steps that lift ships up from sea level and down again. This print by Joseph Pennell shows a group of workers being hoisted out of the locks during construction.

The Reason to Build

Why did people build this mammoth canal? Using the canal, ships save about 9,000 miles (14,500 km) on the journey from New York City to San Francisco because they no longer have to go around the southern tip of South America. Ships going between Europe and Asia save thousands of miles as well. Large numbers of ships, carrying millions of tons of cargo, still use the canal every year to shorten their journeys.

A Big Story

The story of the Panama Canal is more than just one of engineering. It is the story of dreams and the dedicated individuals who made those dreams come true. It is the story of financial disasters, political shenanigans, and medical breakthroughs. Finally, it is the story of the time when the United States first exerted power on the world stage.

A 2002 photograph of the Panama Canal shows vessels of all sizes on the busy route. Between twelve thousand and thirteen thousand ships use the Panama Canal every year.

An Important Historic Event

"The creation of the Panama Canal was far more than a vast, unprecedented feat of engineering. It was a profoundly important historic event and a sweeping human drama. . . . It marked a score of advances in engineering, government planning, [and] labor relations. . . . It was both the crowning constructive effort . . . of the Victorian Era and the first grandiose and assertive show of American power at the dawn of a new century. And yet the passage of the first ship through the canal . . . marked the resolution of a dream as old as the voyages of Columbus."

David McCullough, The Path Between the Seas, *1977*

Bridging the Oceans

Vasco Nuñez de Balboa's expedition crossed Panama to see the Pacific Ocean in 1513. Balboa founded Panama's first permanent European settlement during the Spanish colonization of the Americas.

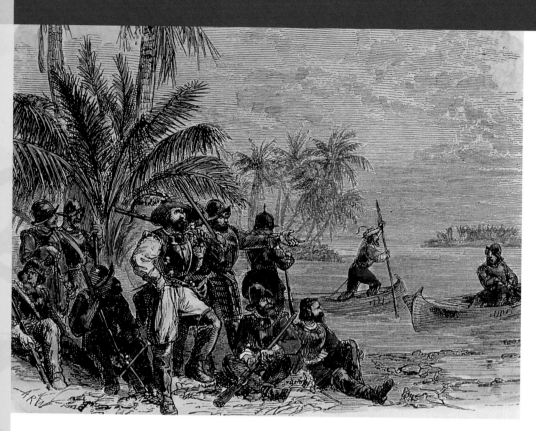

The Isthmus

Panama forms the isthmus—a narrow strip of land connecting two larger landmasses—that links the North American continent (which includes Central America) with the South American continent. What makes Panama important is the fact that it is narrower than any other part of Central America (see the map on page 13).

Claiming the Pacific

The story of the Panama Canal begins with the Spanish exploration of the Americas in the early 1500s. Explorer Vasco Nuñez de Balboa left Spain for the Americas seeking wealth. He ended up on the isthmus of Panama, where Native Americans told him of a nearby "Great Water"—the Pacific Ocean. Hoping to win favor with Spain's king, he led a party on a grueling overland journey. On September 27, 1513, he mounted a ridge and spied the ocean. He claimed its waters and all the lands that touched them for the king.

Conquering the Americas

Around this time, Spain conquered the Aztec Empire of Mexico, gaining rich gold and silver mines. Soon after, Spain's conquest of the Inca Empire in Peru yielded other valuable mines.

Peru's silver had to be transported across dense forests to Spanish ports on the Caribbean Sea or loaded on ships in the Pacific and carried around the southern tip of South America to Spain. Both routes were long and dangerous, and Spanish officials hoped to find a waterway connecting the Atlantic and Pacific Oceans. Unable to find such a waterway, however, they began talking about building a canal across Central America.

Different Routes

The Spanish considered several different places to build a canal. One was across Mexico, where the land tended to be flatter and the rivers more tame. But this route was very long. The middle route crossed what is now southern Nicaragua. The path was shorter than the Mexican route and was also relatively low. In the center of the region lay Lake Nicaragua, a large body of water that ships could navigate, making the job of building a canal easier. A third option was in Panama, from the Chagres River on the Atlantic side to the site of what is now Panama City on the Pacific side. Although much shorter than the other two, this path crossed through difficult land comprising dense rain forests in a hot, wet climate that bred disease.

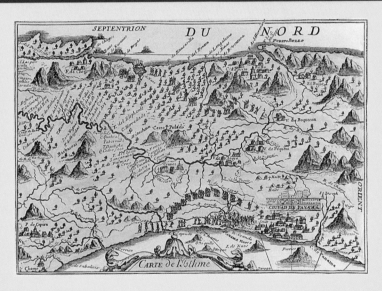

A 1744 European map shows the mountains and forests that make up Panama's landscape.

7

During the mid-1800s, large numbers of optimistic settlers made their way west across North America in wagon trains such as this one. They were led by scouts who protected them from the perils of the journey.

Talk but No Action

In the end, the Spanish did not build a canal in Central America. They feared that doing so would simply make it easier for British ships to sail the seas and raid Spanish treasure ships.

In the early 1800s, various people once again raised the idea of a canal across Central America. Some drew up imaginative plans, but no canal was ever built. No one could agree on a plan, and no country—or group of companies—could raise the huge sums of money needed to carry out the work.

A Growing Country

Meanwhile, a new power was arising in the Americas. By the early 1800s, the United States was pushing westward from the Atlantic coast. Some talked about the nation's "**Manifest Destiny**" to control North America.

While the United States was expanding westward, it also began looking south. Some American leaders began promoting the idea of a transportation route that would cut across Central America.

American Destiny

"The . . . destiny of the American [people] is to subdue the continent—to rush over this vast field to the Pacific Ocean . . . to set the principle of self-government at work . . . to establish a new order in human affairs . . . to teach old nations a new civilization—to confirm the destiny of the human race—to carry the career of mankind to its culminating point . . . to perfect science—to emblazon history with the conquest of peace—to shed a new and resplendent glory upon mankind."

William Gilpin, report to Congress, 1846

Two Treaties

The U.S. government signed two **treaties** related to the idea of creating a route across Central America. The first was signed in 1846 with Colombia, which controlled neighboring Panama. In the treaty, Colombia granted the United States the right to move people and goods across the isthmus of Panama. The United States, in exchange, agreed that it would use force, if ever necessary, to protect Colombia's control over Panama.

The second treaty came four years later with Britain. In this agreement, both countries pledged not to build a canal across

The sea journey from the east coast to the west coast of the United States took months. In the 1846 treaty, the United States gained the right to a land route across Panama, which made the journey much quicker.

Central America without including the other. They also promised that any canal built would not be **fortified**.

The Panama Railroad Company

Efforts to build a canal across the isthmus failed to progress, and some American businessmen began a new approach to the transportation problem in the 1840s. They formed the Panama Railroad Company in 1847, with the aim of building a railroad that linked the Atlantic and Pacific coasts of Panama. They ran into many problems, however. Only 7 miles (11 km) of track were laid before the company ran out of money.

The Gold Rush

Meanwhile, Americans found a new reason to move west. In early 1848, gold was found in California. The discovery spurred thousands of people from the East to go to California, hoping to strike it rich. Many traveled overland, while others went by ship around the tip of South America.

Too Many Emigrants

"There were about seven hundred **emigrants** waiting for passage, when I reached Panama. All the tickets the steamer could possibly receive had been issued and so great was the anxiety to get on, that double price, $600, was frequently paid for a ticket to San Francisco."

Bayard Taylor, Eldorado, *1850*

This illustration shows settlers in California looking for gold. The Gold Rush attracted many thousands of Americans to the West and encouraged the efforts to find new and faster routes from the East.

To cut short the long ocean voyage around South America, ship companies set up a new route, bringing passengers to Panama and leaving them on its Atlantic shore. The gold seekers then had to find their own way across Panama to board other ships on the Pacific coast.

The sudden demand for transportation gave the Panama Railroad's owners—and American investors—new hope. Soon the company raised the funds and, in 1855, completed the train line. Until the end of the 1860s, the railroad carried thousands of people across the isthmus to the West.

Crossing Panama

Although traveling across Panama cut thousands of miles from their trip, gold seekers crossing the isthmus before the railroad was built found it to be a difficult and dangerous journey. The first stretch, from the coast by boat down the Chagres River, was not so bad. The rest of the journey was made on horses or mules through 50 miles

Travelers make the journey through the Panama jungle.

(80 km) of steep passes and dense jungle. (At one point, camels were brought from Africa to carry people across Panama.) Many people caught malaria, yellow fever, or other tropical diseases and died. Other travelers were killed by thieves. Bayard Taylor, a journalist who wrote about the Gold Rush, described the Panama jungle: "The only sounds in that leafy wilderness were the chattering of monkeys as they cracked the palm nuts and the scream of parrots, flying from tree to tree."

Chapter 2

The French Attempt

Looking for a Project

Americans were not the only people looking to improve the route across Panama. Ferdinand de Lesseps was a Frenchman who had masterminded the building of the Suez Canal in North Africa. In the 1870s, he was looking for a new project and eventually settled on the idea of a Central American canal.

The Suez Canal

An aerial view of the Suez Canal shows how it joins the Mediterranean Sea (top) to the Gulf of Suez (bottom), which opens into the Red Sea.

In 1869, a canal in a different part of the world—North Africa—caught public attention. While working as a **diplomat** in Egypt, Ferdinand de Lesseps met a French engineer with a plan for a project that became the Suez Canal. Connecting the Mediterranean Sea and Red Sea, the Suez Canal would—like the Panama Canal—save ships the need to travel great distances. De Lesseps also met Said Pasha, who would become Egypt's ruler. In 1854, Said Pasha gave Ferdinand de Lesseps permission to build the canal.

With persuasive speeches, de Lesseps convinced French people to contribute half of the funds needed for the project. Egypt's government supplied the rest. After ten years of work, a French team completed the Suez Canal. De Lesseps supervised the work until the canal's triumphal opening in 1869. Across France, de Lesseps was hailed as "the Great Frenchman" and "the Great Engineer," although he knew little of engineering. Today, the Suez Canal, which is about 100 miles (160 km) long, is the most heavily used shipping channel in the world.

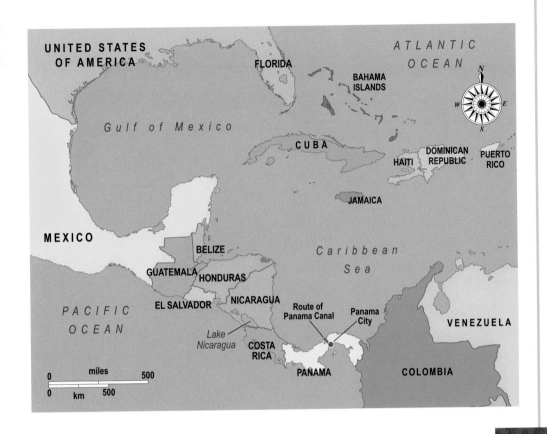

People were undecided about the best place to build a canal in Central America. American engineers told de Lesseps a route across Nicaragua would be easier and cheaper to build, but de Lesseps insisted on the Panama route.

De Lesseps' son Charles warned him not to take on the new project, but the older man insisted. A group of powerful French business and political leaders formed a company and put forward some money. They sent a group to Panama to survey the land, and the group's leader, Lucien Wyse, persuaded Colombia's government to give the French company the right to build a canal.

An International Conference

In 1879, de Lesseps staged an international conference to discuss the idea of a canal. U.S. engineers at the conference favored a route through Nicaragua, but de Lesseps insisted that Panama would be best. He proclaimed that, although skeptics had doubted that he would complete the Suez Canal, he had proven them wrong. People's faith in the old man was great, and the conference quickly approved the Panama route. The crowd also roared its approval when de Lesseps declared that he would lead the effort.

A Warning
"Certainly the Panama project is grandiose . . . but consider the risks those who direct it will run! You succeeded at Suez by a miracle. Should not one be satisfied with accomplishing one miracle in a lifetime?"

Charles de Lesseps, to his father, 1879

13

Raising Money

De Lesseps hoped to persuade thousands of small investors to buy **shares** in the company. They would earn back their money—and more, he said—when the canal began charging **tolls** to ships. Newspapers did little to promote the idea, however. The money only trickled in, and so de Lesseps staged a well-publicized trip to Panama. With great fanfare, he announced the beginning of the project. He paid French journalists to write more favorable stories and made public speeches saying that the Panama Canal would be an easier project than the Suez Canal had been. Believing in the "Great Engineer," about 600,000 people quickly bought shares.

Buying the Panama Railroad

The French had to buy the Panama Railroad because the railroad's agreement allowed it to block any canal. Another

On his arrival in Panama, de Lesseps was greeted in Panama City by a huge crowd under a triumphal arch with his picture at the top.

reason to buy it was that the French wanted to use the railroad to move men and supplies during construction.

As the French plan began to move forward, however, smart investors quickly bought up the railroad's stock. The going price was about $100 a share, but the railroad insisted that the French pay $200 a share. Angry but with little choice, the French company paid the exorbitant price.

The Work

Work on the canal began in 1880. De Lesseps had favored a sea-level canal, like the Suez Canal, instead of one using locks. Such an approach in Panama, however, faced two major obstacles. The canal route had to cross higher land than the Suez Canal had done,

The Panama Railroad ran 49 miles (79 km) from the Gulf of Mexico to Panama City. In addition to passengers, it carried cargo traveling from Asia to Europe and the United States.

and the workers had to dig through rock, not the sand and soft earth of Egypt. Getting down to sea level would be a problem.

Panama posed other problems as well. Dense forests and large swamps were difficult to move through. The warm, wet climate was a perfect breeding ground for mosquitoes, which carry the germs that cause malaria and yellow fever. These deadly diseases killed as many as twenty thousand workers and weakened thousands more.

Panama Plagues

The Panama jungle was a breeding ground for tropical diseases.

Both yellow fever and malaria are caused by tiny germs that are injected into the human body when a mosquito bites a person. Within a few days, a yellow fever victim begins to suffer headache and backache, a high fever, and nausea. People with this disease often die within a week of showing symptoms. Malaria is less likely to kill its victims, but it makes people unable to work and can recur months and even years later.

Doctors did not understand the connection between mosquitoes and either disease until the 1890s. In spite of this, people did develop a treatment for malaria, using quinine made from the bark of the cinchona, a tropical tree. Until the middle 1900s, however, there was no treatment for yellow fever.

16

Mud slides and other problems delayed progress on the French project throughout the 1880s. Here, workers are cutting a channel to divert the fast-flowing Chagres River, but they never succeeded. The problem was solved years later, during the U.S. project, with a huge dam.

The Plan's Collapse

Work progressed less quickly than had been hoped. Laborers weakened by disease could not work as hard. Heavy rains often caused massive mud and rock slides that poured earth into channels that had been dug out. By 1885, de Lesseps was giving higher estimates for the total cost of the project and saying more time would be needed. The company was forced to borrow more and more money. Worse, a French government report issued the next year suggested that the company had to abandon the sea-level approach and build a canal with locks.

In 1887, de Lesseps finally agreed to build locks—after years of saying this was the wrong approach. He campaigned feverishly to convince investors to buy **bonds** so the company could keep working. By late 1888, there was not enough money to continue. In 1889, the canal company declared **bankruptcy**. The French effort was a colossal failure, and all the investors lost their money.

Harsh Words

"This evil doer [de Lesseps] is treated like a hero. . . . But into this affair, which has swallowed up almost a billion and a half [francs], there has been no investigation whatever; not once has this man been asked: 'What have you done with the money?'"

Edouard Dumont, The Last Battle, *1890*

The American Plan

In 1898, U.S. troops entered Ponce, Puerto Rico, to take control of the island during the Spanish-American War. The takeover was one of several U.S. acts of imperialism in the late 1800s.

Looking Abroad

By 1853, the United States had gained control of the whole North American continent south of Canada and north of Mexico. In the late 1800s, the nation had grown richer and—in a military sense—more powerful. Americans began to look beyond their borders for more territory to control. This **imperialism** was spurred in part by economic motives. Control of foreign lands would give the United States the raw materials needed to manufacture goods. Those foreign lands were also home to many people who would buy those goods.

Territory and Trade in the Pacific

In 1898, the United States **annexed** the Hawaiian Islands. That same year, it gained control over Puerto Rico in the Caribbean Sea and Guam and the Philippine Islands in the Pacific Ocean during the **Spanish-American War**. The United States had gained possessions in the Pacific, raising the importance of a canal that would cut travel time between the Pacific and Atlantic Oceans.

Competing with the World

"Within, the home market is secured; but outside, beyond the broad seas, there are the markets of the world, that can be entered or controlled only by a vigorous contest."

Alfred Thayer Mahan, 1890s

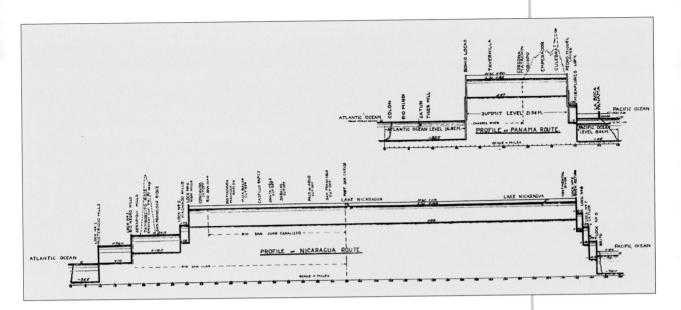

Supporting the idea of a canal was an influential military thinker, Admiral Alfred Thayer Mahan. Mahan had long argued that a canal would allow U.S. companies to compete with European businesses for trade in Asia. He also thought having a canal would make it easier for the U.S. Navy to defend both of the nation's coasts.

Renewed Enthusiasm

Americans were once more deeply interested in a canal across Central America—but where? Many members of the U.S. Congress

The diagram above was prepared during a government study to compare two possible routes for a canal across Central America. The proposed Nicaraguan canal would have been longer but could have made use of the waters of Lake Nicaragua for much of the route.

A New Treaty Overturns an Old One

To build a canal in Panama, the United States had to overcome a political obstacle. In the Clayton-Bulwer Treaty of 1850, the country had pledged not to build and control a canal in Central America without Britain. In 1901, however, U.S. Secretary of State John Hay was able to work out a new agreement—the Hay-Pauncefote Treaty—with the British government, in which Britain agreed that the United States could construct and control a canal in Central America as long as it was open to all nations on equal terms.

One of the main concerns in deciding where to build the canal was the high death rate in Panama during the French project. A 1904 magazine illustrated that concern with a cover showing "Death" hovering over the Panama Canal.

preferred the Nicaragua route. The huge lake in the middle would mean less digging. Disease was less of a problem there than in Panama, and the idea of a Panama route was already stained by the French failure.

In 1899, Congress formed a commission to study both routes. In 1901, the Walker Commission issued its report backing the Nicaraguan route. The commission said, however, it would be better to take advantage of the start the French had made in Panama but that the price was too high. The French canal company had put a price of $109 million on its equipment and rights to the route.

A Decision Is Made

Two determined men were still backing the Panama route. One was an influential New York lawyer named William Nelson Cromwell, hired by the French canal company of France as its agent in the United States. Cromwell urged the French company to drop its price to just $40 million.

A Lightning Intellect

"[Cromwell] can smile as sweetly as a society belle and at the same time deal a blow at a business foe that ties him in a hopeless tangle of financial knots. . . . [He] has an intellect that works like a flash of lightning, and it swings about with the agility of an acrobat."

New York World, *1908*

The other man was Philippe Bunau-Varilla, a French engineer committed to what he called the "Great Adventure of Panama." He knew that the French company only had rights to build the canal until 1904. If it did not sell the rights by then, the investors would lose everything. Bunau-Varilla and Cromwell finally persuaded the French investors to drop their price.

With the price lowered, the commission issued a new report in January 1902, saying the canal should be built in Panama. In a close vote in Congress that same year, the Panama site was approved.

Philippe Bunau-Varilla was the driving force behind the plan to build a canal across Panama. This photograph shows him on a ship in 1914, two days before the grand opening of the canal.

Philippe Bunau-Varilla (1859—1940)

Born to a poor family in France, Philippe Bunau-Varilla won a scholarship to an engineering school. In his last year there, he heard Ferdinand de Lesseps lecture on the French Panama Canal project. His imagination fired by the idea, Bunau-Varilla joined the canal-building team and was put in charge of an important section of the work. After becoming ill in Panama, Bunau-Varilla returned to France. He worked on other projects but never lost his interest in Panama. When de Lesseps' effort collapsed, Bunau-Varilla joined others in forming the New Panama Canal Company, which bought the French equipment in the hope of restarting the canal. He played an important role in getting the U.S. government to decide to build in Panama. After the canal project ended, Bunau-Varilla fought for France in World War I. He lost a leg in one battle but survived, and he remained active until his death.

A cartoon from 1903 shows President Roosevelt refusing to give in to Colombia's demands for more money. In the end, the Colombians turned down the American treaty and dollars.

Negotiating with Colombia

The United States and Colombia quickly negotiated a treaty that called for the Americans to pay $10 million in advance to lease the land for the canal and then an additional $250,000 each year. The treaty was widely disliked in Colombia, however, where people felt it was overly generous to the Americans. As a result, in the summer of 1903, the Senate of Colombia rejected the agreement. U.S. President Theodore Roosevelt fumed.

Man with a Plan

"A MAN, A PLAN, A CANAL, PANAMA."

*A famous **palindrome** about President Roosevelt and the Panama Canal*

Panama Stirs

The people of Panama, meanwhile, had resented Colombia's control over their land for many years. They had rebelled a number of times during the 1800s and now saw a chance to break free of Colombia with American help. Bunau-Varilla, hoping to save his investment, played a role. He met with U.S. diplomats and with Roosevelt and talked about the possibility that Panamanians might rebel to win their independence. The Americans, while they could not actively support a revolution, made no sign that they disapproved.

Declaring Independence

Bunau-Varilla told the rebels in Panama that he could ensure

HELD UP THE WRONG MAN

A 1911 photograph shows people celebrating Independence Day in Panama City.

U.S. support. In return, the Frenchman wanted to be the person to negotiate a treaty for canal rights.

On November 3, 1903, the rebels declared Panama's independence. Colombian troops landed to try and regain control, but their commanders were seized. The Colombian soldiers—who had not

Big Stick Diplomacy

In 1900, President Theodore Roosevelt was quoted as saying, "I have always been fond of the West African proverb: 'Speak softly and carry a big stick; you will go far.'" Panama was not the only example of Teddy Roosevelt carrying his big stick. In 1905, Roosevelt announced a new policy: If the countries of Latin America did not maintain order, the United States would send troops to impose order. Roosevelt and later presidents did not hesitate to do this. In another show of strength, the U.S. Navy sailed around the world from 1907 to 1909 on what was called a "goodwill cruise." There was no doubt that Roosevelt was showing other countries just how powerful the United States was.

been paid for a long time by Colombia's government—were given money to persuade them not to fight.

U.S. warships were already in the area. The next day, U.S. troops landed to make sure there was no more fighting.

The Treaty with Panama

Within days, the United States recognized the new government of Panama. Bunau-Varilla wrote a new treaty giving the United States the right to an area called the Canal Zone and to build a canal there. The Americans received **sovereignty** over the Canal Zone, which is more than they would have received under the treaty with the Colombian government.

On November 18, Bunau-Varilla—on behalf of Panama—and Secretary of State John Hay for the United States signed the treaty. The Panamanians were appalled by what Bunau-Varilla had given away but accepted the treaty because they needed the $10 million payment that the United States had offered. In February 1904, the U.S. Senate approved the Hay-Bunau-Varilla Treaty.

Taking Over

With the treaty approved, the United States paid Panama its $10 million, and Panama gave the Americans control of the Canal Zone. Soon after, the American government paid $40 million to France's New Panama

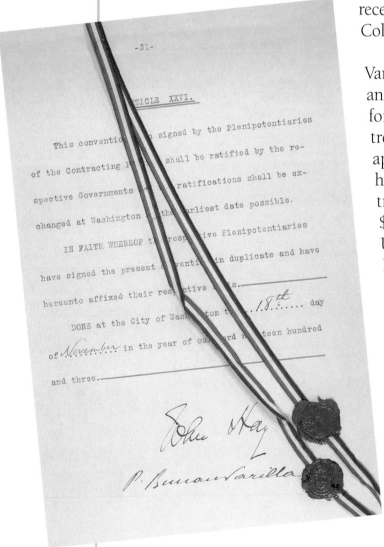

-31-

TICLE XXVI.

This conventio... signed by the Plenipotentiaries of the Contracting ... shall be ratified by the respective Governments ... ratifications shall be exchanged at Washington ... the earliest date possible.

IN FAITH WHEREOF the respective Plenipotentiaries have signed the present ... in duplicate and have hereunto affixed their respective ...

DONE at the City of Washington the ..18th...... day of November in the year of our ...rd n...teen hundred and three.

Canal Company. That gave the United States control of all the work done to date and of the buildings and equipment still in Panama. There were hundreds of buildings, including offices, warehouses to store supplies, housing for workers to live in, and hospitals.

There was also equipment—locomotives, **steam shovels**, and other machinery. Some of it had been cared for and could still work. Some, however, had been sitting in Panama's wet rain forest for twenty years or more and had turned to rust.

Roosevelt appointed seven men to a canal board named the Isthmian Canal Commission (ICC) to run the work. The ICC took control of the Canal Zone and everything in it.

The U.S.-Panama Treaty
"[Panama grants the United States] all the rights, power, and authority within the zone mentioned . . . which the United States would possess and exercise if it were the sovereign . . . to the entire exclusion of the exercise by the Republic of Panama of any such sovereign rights, power or authority."

Hay-Bunau-Varilla Treaty, 1903

Under the Hay-Bunau-Varilla Treaty, the United States gained the right to protect and fortify the Canal Zone. This poster encouraged men to enlist for duty in Panama.

Chapter 4

Building the Canal

Getting Started

In 1905, engineer John Stevens became chief engineer of the Panama Canal project. Stevens realized that the first task was not to begin digging but to *prepare* for the digging. He believed that the secret to building the canal was to have enough train service to remove the debris that was being dug out.

The first task, therefore, was to replace the old Panama Railroad with wider, heavier tracks that could handle larger, more powerful locomotives and longer trains. Stevens also had multiple tracks built so trains could serve all points along the canal. At the Culebra **Cut**, for instance, tracks were laid at different levels so that steam shovels could work at different depths of the cut at the same time.

Making the Decision

The U.S. government had still not decided whether to build a sea-level canal or a lock canal—the same issue that had challenged the French. Stevens came to believe the canal had to have locks, but in 1906, an advisory commission recommended that it be built at sea

The complex rail system introduced by chief engineer John Stevens included 450 miles (724 km) of track, about 9 miles (14.5 km) for each mile of canal. The tracks snaked back and forth along the canal route on several levels, enabling trains to remove huge amounts of debris. The total amount of soil moved by the French and U.S. efforts combined was four times the amount dug to make the 100-mile (160-km) Suez Canal.

President Roosevelt took a personal interest in the huge engineering project. On his visit to Panama in 1906, he was photographed (in white suit and hat) inside one of the steam shovels used for canal construction.

level. Stevens went to Washington to explain that a lock system would not only be easier, cheaper, and faster to build, but easier and cheaper to run. The ICC and President Roosevelt supported his view. In June 1906, Congress approved the locks. At last, the engineers knew what kind of canal they were building.

A New Leader

Late in 1906, President Roosevelt traveled to Panama to tour the work. He was impressed by the progress that had been made, and before departing he gave a pep talk to the engineers. "This is one of the great works of the world," he told them.

Stevens, however, was thoroughly tired of this great work. The following January, he wrote a long and somewhat critical letter to Roosevelt. While not stating that he was resigning, Stevens did ask for a rest. The president—angry at the tone and feeling that Stevens had lost his energy and drive—quickly replied that his resignation was accepted. Stevens was gone.

Safer, Quicker, Cheaper
"[A lock canal] will provide a safer and quicker passage for ships. . . .
It will provide, beyond question, the best solution to the vital problem of how safely to care for the floodwaters of the Chagres. . . . Its cost of operation [and] maintenance . . . will be much less than any sea-level canal."

John Stevens, testifying to a Senate committee, 1906

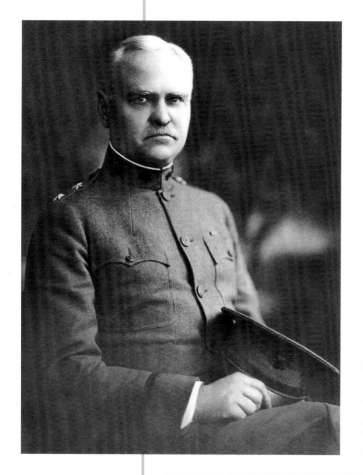

The canal project got a new leader, an army engineer named George Goethals. Roosevelt gave Goethals complete power over the seven-man ICC.

Disease and Death

The French effort to build a canal across Panama had been hurt badly by yellow fever and malaria. The United States, therefore, sent army doctor William Gorgas to try to put an end to the problem.

In the end, Gorgas had success against many diseases. By December 1905, yellow fever was gone from Panama. Malaria rates dropped from 205 cases in the period 1907–1908 to only 14 in the period 1913–1914.

Lt. Col. George Washington Goethals took over as Panama Canal Chief Engineer after the departure of Stevens in 1907. He proved to be an able administrator and was extremely careful with money.

George Goethals (1858–1928)

George Goethals was educated at the U.S. Military Academy at West Point, where he learned engineering. An excellent student, he graduated second in his class and was elected president of the student body. Goethals spent the next two decades working on various army engineering projects, many involving canals and harbor improvements. He was thus ably prepared for taking charge of the Panama project. Goethals also had influence: In 1903, he had been named to a special board of army officers who served in Washington, D.C. After the canal was finished, Goethals was put in charge of the Canal Zone as governor and served in that post until 1917. After helping in the U.S. Army's efforts in World War I, he retired and ran an engineering company until his death.

In fact, deaths from all causes were far lower than during the French effort, although they were still high. About 5,600 people lost their lives while working on the U.S. project. A large number of workers died from pneumonia in 1907, but after that year, construction accidents were the main threat to the lives of laborers.

Fighting Fevers

William Gorgas had served in Cuba during the Spanish-American War of 1898, a time when the link between mosquitoes and certain diseases was finally proven. He had led the effort to destroy mosquitoes in Havana, Cuba, and he was determined to do the same in Panama. At first, Gorgas could not do much because his superiors did not believe that mosquitoes were the problem and so would not give him the supplies he asked for. In 1905, yellow fever broke out. While it did not kill large numbers of people, it did cause a panic.

A Panama Canal worker sprays oil on an open ditch in the Canal Zone.

Gorgas then got the go-ahead to set teams to work clearing the land on either side of the canal. They dug nearly 2,000 miles (3,200 km) of ditches so that swamps could be drained. They put a coating of oil on areas of standing water to smother mosquitoes hatching from eggs deposited on the water. One member of the team also developed a spray that could be used to kill newly hatched mosquitoes. In the cities, Gorgas's men paved streets so that there were no longer pools of water for female mosquitoes to lay eggs in.

Facilities and Entertainment

To keep the skilled workers happy, the ICC provided them with some entertainment. Clubhouses had dance halls, libraries, billiard rooms, and bowling alleys. Movies—then a new form of amusement—were brought in from the United States, as were performing groups. Land was set aside for baseball fields, and workers were urged to form teams. American workers were also encouraged to bring their wives and families, and schools and stores were built in the Canal Zone.

The Workers

The death rates were higher among the black workers than among whites. One reason for that difference was that blacks from the West Indies did much of the heavy manual labor. They provided the bulk of the workforce, around three-fourth of the total. The next largest group was Americans, who made up about 15 percent of the workforce. The rest came from European countries—mostly Italy and

These men were drilling holes to place dynamite for blasting through rock. There were many dangerous jobs to be done on the canal, and the accident rate was high.

Drilling holes for blasting at Culebra, Panama Canal.

Spain—and many other nations, including India. At one point during the project, the ICC employed more than forty thousand workers.

Inequality in the Workforce

Workers were treated differently depending on where they came from. American workers were paid in U.S. gold dollars; the rest were paid in silver dollars from Panama. Americans filled the more advanced positions and had the highest wages, but European laborers still earned more than the workers from the West Indies did. American workers had decent housing to live in and could eat in real dining halls, whereas the European workers ate in food tents and the West Indians were fed out of kitchen shacks. Unlike the white workers, black workers had to provide their own housing, which was of poor quality because of the low wages they earned.

Most workers labored on building the canal, but there were countless other jobs. Some worked to build and maintain the houses and other buildings

Thousands of men, such as those above, worked on the canal at any one time. The Commissary Department provided huge volumes of food, including 6 million loaves of bread in one year. Some cooking was done over campfires (below) near where the men were working.

This map shows the area of the Canal Zone and the various sites along the Panama Canal route.

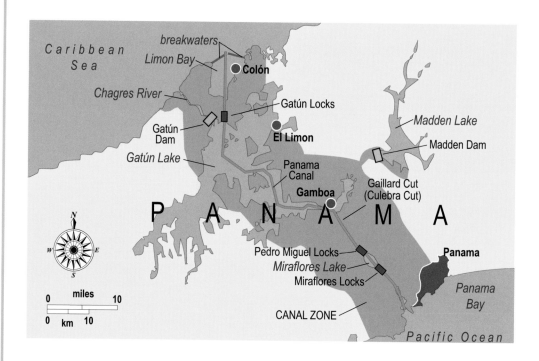

needed by this vast workforce. Others moved supplies in and around the Canal Zone. Some worked on the medical staff or did administrative work.

Damming the River

The first construction task was to **dam** the wild Chagres River, near the Atlantic side of the canal. If this was not done, heavy rains would turn the river into a raging force that would endanger ships using the canal. The French had never decided on a dam, the only solution to the problem. The Americans made it a priority. Gatún Dam would be huge in size—1.5 miles (2.4 km) long, 0.5 miles (0.8 km) thick at the bottom, and tapering to 30 feet (9 meters) at the top.

Gatún Dam served two purposes: not only did it tame the river, but it also provided power. A **hydroelectric** power plant was built near the dam that used the flowing water of the river to make electrical power. The power plant generated enough energy to power the locks, the electric trains used to pull ships through the locks, and all the lights needed in the Canal Zone. This use of electricity was an innovation—when the work began, electric power was still relatively new. At the time, only one factory in the United States ran on electric power.

The enormous dam created a new lake—when completed, Gatún Lake was the world's largest artificial lake. It has a surface area of over 160 square miles (414 square kilometers).

The Culebra Cut

Next to the Chagres River, the greatest problem in building the canal was to cut through an area of highlands near the Pacific end. The French had failed on this 9-mile (14.5-km) stretch because Panama's

Gatún Lake was created in what was once the valley of the Chagres River. Today, ships follow the canal's shipping channel across the lake from Gatún Locks to Gamboa.

heavy rains repeatedly washed dirt down from the highlands onto the work area and threatened to doom the project. The Americans were forced to make the cut through the highlands, called the Culebra Cut, much wider than they had planned—only in that way could they take away enough dirt to prevent further mud slides. The final width of the cut at the top was 1,800 feet (550 m), nearly three times the original width. The work took years and was not completed until just a few months before the canal opened.

Solving the Problems

Despite having to do more digging, the Americans succeeded where the French had failed for three reasons. First, the U.S. team used

A Great Spectacle

"He who did not see the Culebra Cut during the mighty work of excavation missed one of the great spectacles of all ages. . . . From its crest on a working day you looked down upon a mighty rift in the earth's crust, at the base of which pigmy engines and ant-like forms were rushing to and fro without seeming plan or reason."

Willis John Abbot, Panama and the Canal in Picture and Prose, *1913*

higher-powered steam shovels that could scoop out five times the dirt that the French shovels managed. Second, when they hit rock, the Americans—unlike the French—had dynamite to blast it apart. Third, Stevens' rail network enabled them to remove far more dirt than the French system could handle.

Much of the material taken from the Culebra Cut was put to use. Rock was dumped into the oceans outside the two canal entrances to help build **breakwaters**. Dirt from the cut was taken by train to Gatún, where it was used to build the dam.

Building the Locks

Another crucial task was building the locks. Each lock was huge, 110 feet (33.5 m) wide and 1,100 feet (335 m) long. The bottom and sides were made of concrete, poured on the site. The steel gates for the locks, weighing about 400 tons, were made in the United States and shipped to Panama to be installed.

The first concrete was poured for Gatún Locks in 1909. Work on the twelve locks continued until completion in 1913.

The locks were designed to work easily, using gravity to let water flow in from above or out from below. This elegant design lessened the need for moving parts. The designers put as many as seventy valves in the bottoms of the locks to allow water to flow in and out. This meant water would be distributed evenly throughout the lock, resulting in a calm journey for ships from one level to another.

An Engineering Feat

Statistics show just how impressive the engineering work in Panama really was. In their ten years of work, the Americans excavated 232 million cubic yards (177 million cubic meters) of dirt and rocks. Nearly 10 percent of the total was the removal of mud slides.

Each lock stretched the length of five city blocks, and its side walls soared to the height of a six-story building. Nothing on that scale had ever been made of concrete before, but the builders of the Panama Canal made twelve of them.

The cost was huge as well— $352 million was paid by the United States, including the $50 million paid to Panama and to the French company. This cost was about three times the original estimate. The Culebra Cut alone cost $90 million, about one-quarter of the cost of building the canal.

The monumental Gatún Dam was an engineering triumph and is still one of the world's largest dams.

Completing the Work

In 1913, as the project neared its end, morale soared. Work on the locks on the Pacific side was finished first, followed by the Gatún Locks on the Atlantic side. In June 1913, the dam was completed and the last gates closed so that Gatún Lake would fill. Eventually, the lake reached the desired height of 85 feet (26 m). In September, the locks were tested for the first time with a vessel—a tiny tugboat. Everything worked flawlessly.

Within days of the lock test, there was a scare when a strong earthquake shook Panama. Goethals was pleased to report no damage to the canal itself. Soon after, temporary **dikes**, built along the canal to hold back the water flow during construction, were blown up, and the Culebra Cut began filling with water. The channel in the cut was still not usable by large ships, however—it needed to be **dredged**. That work was finished in December 1913.

The first complete journey through the canal was made in February 1914 by a ship called the *Panama*. A smaller escort vessel accompanies the *Panama* through the Culebra Cut during that trial run. After the *Panama*, other vessels made test runs through the canal to prepare for its grand opening in August 1914.

Using the Canal

Opening Ceremonies

On August 15, 1914, the Panama Canal officially opened when the *Ancon*, a cargo ship, made the journey through the canal. The ship carried various officials, including Panama's president and the U.S. ambassador. Goethals was not on board. He rode on the train line alongside the canal, stopping at each lock to make sure everything was in order before the ship arrived. The ship easily made the trip in less than ten hours.

Philippe Bunau-Varilla, another person who had done so much to make the canal a reality, actually traveled through the canal before the *Ancon*. He rode aboard the *Cristobal,* a ship that made a test voyage through the canal two days before.

On opening day, August 15, 1914, the *Ancon* enters the Pedro Miguel Locks. From there, the ship descended to Miraflores Lake and then went down once more in the Miraflores Locks to ocean level, 8 miles (13 km) from the Pacific end of the canal.

Small electric engines, called "mules," run along either side of the locks in the Panama Canal. The engines of all large ships are shut off, and four to twelve mules pull the ships through the lock system with towing cables.

Path Between the Seas

Ten years or so after it opened, the Panama Canal was handling five thousand ships a year. By the 1970s, about fifteen thousand ships were passing through each year, as lights were installed and ships were allowed to make the journey at night. As a result, ships passed

Protecting the Locks

The canal's operators have safeguards to protect the all-important locks by blocking ships from entering at such high speeds that they hit the gates and damage them. Huge chains are strung across the passage as ships approach. If the ship is traveling at a slow enough speed, the chain will go slack and fall into the water. If the ship is going too fast, however, the chain will pull taut, slow the ship down, and eventually stop it. Should a ship break the chain and plow through the first set of gates for each lock, another gate 50 feet (15 m) farther on can stop it.

"The canal is so short, with great variables in tides on the Pacific side and with so many narrow twists and turns, such sudden changes in weather and wind, that if I look away for even three seconds, we could be out of the channel and on a sandbar."

Pilot Edgar Tejada, on steering ships through the Panama Canal, 1999

through the canal at the rate of nearly two per hour every day of the year.

Traveling the Canal

When ships prepare to enter the canal, their captains must hand over the steering to pilots. These experienced workers have the most prestigious jobs on the canal. They guide the ships along the channel from one end of the canal to the other and in and out of the locks.

Only small ships steam into the locks under their own power. Larger, heavier ships are towed through the locks by the electrical engines alongside the waterway.

It takes 52 million gallons (197 million liters) of water to fill each of the huge locks—enough to supply water for a day to a city of about one million people. Since filling the locks requires so much water,

Pilots take over vessels while they are still in the deep waters of Limon Bay or Panama Bay. They have complete control throughout the canal trip.

more than one smaller ship moving in the same direction will enter a lock at the same time if possible.

Change of Ownership

Throughout the twentieth century, many Panamanians remained angry over the terms of the 1903 treaty. Panama and the United States finally agreed to two new treaties in 1977. In one, the United States agreed that Panama had sovereignty over the Canal Zone—this issue had bothered many in Panama for a long time. The treaty also stated that the United States would continue operating the canal until the end of 1999. Then, Panama would take control of the canal, and all U.S. military forces would leave the Canal Zone.

In the second treaty, the two nations agreed to maintain the canal's neutrality. It was also agreed that only Panama can post military forces in the Canal Zone, but U.S. soldiers can be sent to the canal to ensure that it remains open in a military emergency.

The Canal Zone, although ruled by the United States, was home to many native Panamanians. During construction of the Panama Canal, daily life continued as usual in Panama—these women used the canal to do their laundry.

Taking Control

"I feel very, very happy that my country's finally becoming whole again, that we're going to be a sovereign, a free nation, that we're not going to have any more foreign troops in Panama, and I think that the future is a challenge, but the Panamanian people are undoubtedly up to it."

Juan Carlos Navarro, mayor of Panama City, 1999

Conclusion

Today, Panama City has a population of more than 1.2 million. The city's economy is closely linked to the canal.

The Impact of the Panama Canal

The Panama Canal spurred trade and created wealth for many countries by making the transportation of goods so much cheaper than before. In saving thousands of miles of travel, shippers could save thousands of dollars, too.

The canal also boosted Panama's **economy**. Canal workers and U.S. soldiers stationed in the Canal Zone earned good wages and used their earnings to help Panamanian businesses grow. The canal even became a destination for tourists, who enjoy making the eight- to ten-hour journey on comfortable cruise liners. Today, much of Panama's economy is based on industries—including transportation, storage, communications, banking, and tourism—connected with the canal.

Improvements

Today's canal is not the same as the one completed in 1914. In the 1930s, work was completed on another dam—the Madden Dam— east of the canal. This dam helps control the flow of water into

Gatún Lake. The dam is also used to generate electrical power used by the canal. In the 1970s, the Culebra Cut (which has since been renamed the Gaillard Cut) was made broader and deeper. It was made wider and deeper yet again in the 1990s. As a result, even the largest ships that go through the Panama Canal can pass each other in the cut while traveling in opposite directions, which lessens delays.

The ceremonial handover of the canal from U.S. to Panamanian control took place on December 14, 1999, in front of a ship decorated for the celebration.

Fewer Ships

Since the 1970s, when traffic on the Panama Canal reached its peak, use of the canal has fallen. Increasing numbers of ships have been built that are too large to fit in the locks. Still, more than twelve thousand ships a year traverse the canal, and it remains a vital world waterway.

The Legacy of Building the Panama Canal

When it began building the Panama Canal, the United States was just beginning to play a role in the world. Completing this work—a task at which the French had failed—helped give Americans new confidence in their abilities and power.

   The canal also became a vital interest for the United States to protect, and its existence led the nation to take a far more active role in the **Western Hemisphere**. Over the years, U.S. interventions in that region led many Latin Americans to mistrust and fear the United States. Lingering anger over the canal treaty with Panama did not help the problem, and many nations in Central and South America viewed the United States as the region's bully. The 1977 revised treaty between Panama and the United States helped improve the situation, but relations between the United States and its Latin American neighbors remain uneasy.

Time Line

1513	▪	Vasco Nuñez de Balboa becomes the first European to see Pacific Ocean.
1846	▪	In a treaty with Colombia, United States gains the right to move people and goods across the isthmus of Panama and agrees to protect Colombia's control of Panama.
1850	▪	In Clayton-Bulwer Treaty, United States and Britain pledge to cooperate in building any canal across Central America.
1855	▪	Panama Railroad is completed.
1879	▪	Ferdinand de Lesseps holds a conference to discuss building a Central American canal.
1880	▪	French effort to dig the canal begins.
1889	▪	French canal company declares bankruptcy, and work ceases.
1901	▪	In Hay-Pauncefote Treaty, Britain agrees that United States can build and control a canal in Central America.
1902	▪	U.S. Senate approves a canal route in Panama.
1903	▪	January 22: United States and Colombia negotiate a treaty giving the United States the right to build a canal in Panama.
		August 12: Colombian Senate rejects the Panama Canal treaty.
		November 3: Panama declares independence.
		November 6: United States recognizes Panama's independence.
		November 18: Hay-Bunau-Varilla treaty with Panama gives United States the right to build Panama Canal.
		December 2: Panama's new government reluctantly approves Hay-Bunau-Varilla Treaty.
1904	▪	Feb. 23: U.S. Senate approves treaty with Panama.
		May 2: United States buys holdings of New Panama Canal Company of France.
		May 5: Panama hands Canal Zone over to United States.
1905	▪	John Stevens is appointed chief engineer of Panama Canal project.
1906	▪	Senate approves plan for a lock canal.
1907	▪	George Goethals replaces Stevens as head of the project.
1909	▪	First concrete floor is laid for Gatún Locks.
1913	▪	Work is completed on locks, Gatún Dam, and Culebra Cut.
1914	▪	August 15: Panama Canal officially opens.
1977	▪	United States and Panama sign two new treaties.
1999	▪	Panama takes control of the Panama Canal.

Glossary

annex: take control of a country or region and make it officially part of another nation.

bankruptcy: state in which a company loses control of its finances and property because of its debts.

bond: certificate that promises to pay or pay back a certain amount of money by a certain date.

breakwater: barrier built in the sea near a harbor to block high waves from entering the harbor.

canal: manmade waterway.

cut: manmade or natural channel carved through land.

dam: stop or control the flow of water; and the structure that stops and controls a river, often creating an artificial lake.

dike: wall built to hold back the flow of water.

diplomat: person who represents his or her nation in another nation.

dredge: cleaning loose soil out of a ship channel to deepen it.

economy: system of producing and distributing goods and services.

emigrant: person who leaves his or her country to go and live somewhere else.

fortify: build forts or strengthen existing structures to protect against attack.

hydroelectric: electric energy generated by harnessing the flow of water.

imperialism: expansion by a nation, often by conquering or using force to gain control of the government and economy of another country. The 1800s were a time of European and U.S. imperialism.

lock: mechanism in a canal that allows boats to be raised or lowered from a body of water flowing at one level to another body of water that is flowing at a lower or higher level.

manifest: obviously true and easily recognizable. When Americans used the phrase "Manifest Destiny," they meant it was obviously their destiny to take over the continent.

palindrome: word or phrase that is spelled the same both backward and forward.

share: one of a number of equal parts into which a company's stock (or value) is divided. People can buy part ownership in a company by buying shares.

sovereignty: right to rule over an area.

Spanish-American War: war between the United States and Spain in 1898.

steam shovel: machine that uses steam power to carve soil and loose rock out of the ground.

toll: payment made to use a road or waterway.

treaty: agreement made between two or more people or groups after negotiation.

Western Hemisphere: half of the Earth that includes the continents of North and South America and surrounding oceans.

Further Information

Books

Gaines, Ann Graham. *The Panama Canal in American History* (In American History). Enslow, 1999.

Green, Carl R. *The Spanish-American War*. Enslow, 2002.

Hakim, Joy. *An Age of Extremes* (History of US). Oxford University Press Children's Books, 2002.

Kraft, Betsy Harvey. *Theodore Roosevelt: Champion of the American Spirit*. Clarion, 2003.

Smith, Bonnie G. *Imperialism: A History in Documents* (Pages from History). Oxford University Press Children's Books, 2000.

Web Sites

www.pancanal.com Official web site of the organization that runs the canal has information on its current operations.

www.sil.si.edu/Exhibitions/Make-the-Dirt-Fly/ Smithsonian Institution web site has great information and images explaining the building of the canal.

www.theodoreroosevelt.org Web site devoted to the life and achievements of President Theodore Roosevelt.

Useful Addresses

The Panama Canal Museum
7985 113th Street
Suite 100
Seminole, FL 33772-4785
Telephone: (727) 394-9338

Index